MY BROTHER IS NOT GETTING BETTER

Written by:
Vanessa Ya Lopez

Illustrated by:
Joy Anne Nicolas

Azalea Art Press
Sonoma . California

© Vanessa Ya Lopez, 2024
All rights reserved.

ISBN: 978-1-943471-82-9

Cover design
and illustrations
by Joy Anne Nicolas

*To our dads
Orlando and Albert
who cultivated love and compassion
in us from day one
so that we could one day
share it with you.*

Anyone who does anything to help a child in his life is a hero.

— Fred Rogers

A Note for Adults:

The hope for this book is that it may serve as a tool to begin hard conversations with children about loss.

Talking about death with children in an honest way, though painful, can have a positive impact on a child's future coping and understanding of grief.

Normalizing feelings and being present are the first steps in supporting young children. Reading this book together is one way to launch into these important conversations.

Hi. My name is Luna.

I have been feeling really sad and scared.

My brother, Lucca,
has been in the hospital for a long time.
My mom says he is not getting better.

I don't understand why.

Usually, people go to the hospital
when their bodies are sick or hurt
and when they get better, they go home.

Parent Tip: This is an opportunity to talk about why a sibling might be in the hospital: an accident, an operation, a premature baby, or other less serious things.

Why hasn't Lucca come home yet?
I miss him.

My dad tells me my
brother's lungs
are sick.

He says Lucca is
tired and weak
because he can't breathe
on his own.

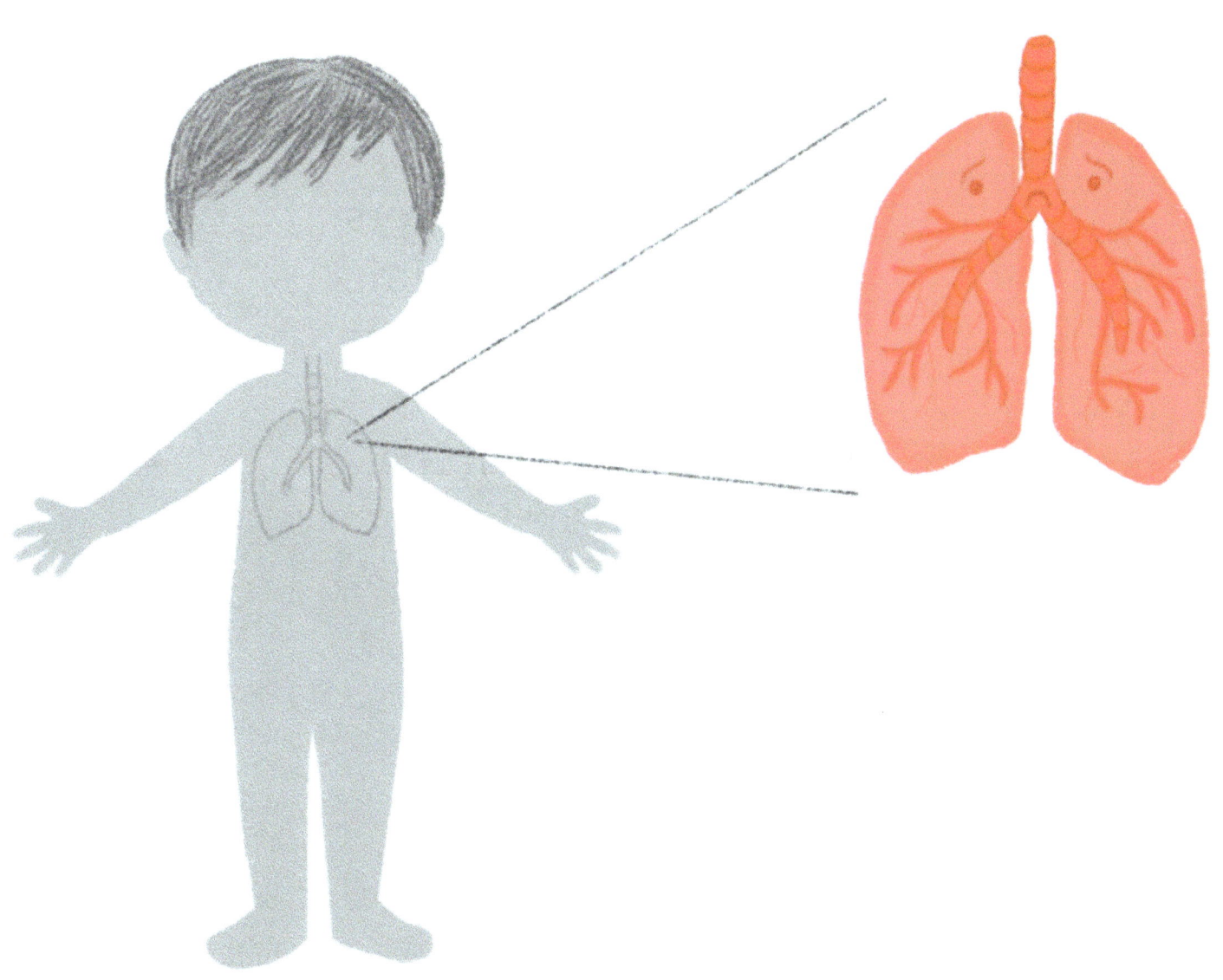

My dad says the doctors
have tried to help him
with different medicines
and machines,
but nothing is helping.

He is still sick.

Parent Tip: Use concrete language. Follow the child's lead when providing information, explaining new information in segments, and not necessarily all at once, especially if the child is not asking.

I want things to go back to the way they were.

I want us to hunt for heart rocks after school, find secret tree swings, make blanket forts,

and eat stacks and stacks of pancakes.

The doctors say
that my brother is dying.

Dying?

I thought only old people
or animals that ran into the street died —
not little brothers.

Parent Tip: Try using concrete words such as "die/death" instead of "passed" or "lost." Death is abstract and children sometimes think the person could come back, which can cause confusion.

My mom says that sometimes kids die too.

Tears roll down her cheeks.

I jump up and hug her.

Parent Tip: This is a good time to reference any experience the sibling has had with death; whether a pet, a grandparent, or something observed in nature.

No! I don't believe my mom.

It feels like my brother and I were just playing video games.

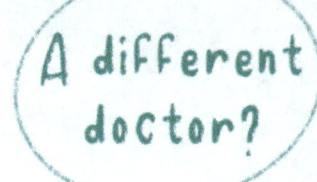

There must be something we can do.

We can't just let him die.

The next few days are hard.

"Our hearts are hurting too, Luna,"
my dad whispers.

Parent Tip: Sometimes words are not as important as your presence. Being a quiet presence is sometimes enough, especially when you are unsure of what to say.

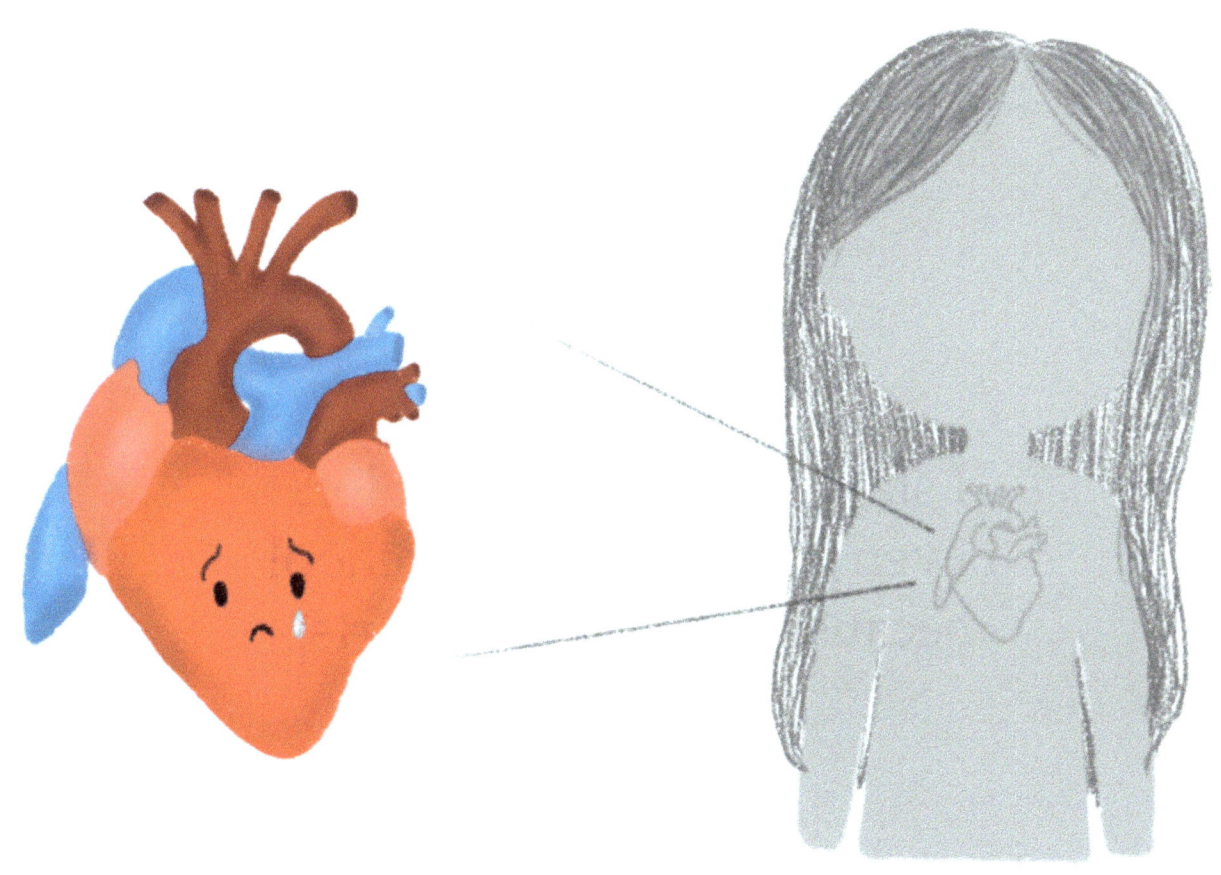

Parent Tip: At different stages of development, kids may try to exert control over situations that are out of their and your control. The best solution is to listen. Giving them opportunities for control in their day-to-day life whenever possible can be helpful.

I stay quiet and sleep a lot.
I even miss one day of school
because my stomach hurts.

Parent Tip: Under stress, some children may experience physical symptoms (headaches or upset stomachs, etc.) as they process their feelings. This is common.

We are going to visit my brother today.
My parents tell me I can say goodbye.

They say his body is getting weaker
and he is getting sicker.

I don't want to tell my brother goodbye.

I am not ready for him to die.
He is still so little.

I spend a few hours
in my brother's hospital room.

It smells clean
like when my mom cleans the house.

Parent Tip: Provide some choices and make sure the sibling has opportunities to interact/touch the patient if they choose. Ensure they also have space to step away, if or when they need a break, if it's too overwhelming. Every child reacts differently.

I talk to his nurse, Abbie, and I even meet a Child Life Specialist.

Parent Tip: Ask your hospital for support from the Child Life Specialists. They can help prepare for the sibling's visit and be present to aid in both the sibling's and patient's coping. Provide choices and specific jobs for the sibling during the visit to help keep them engaged.

The Child Life Specialist talks about
what is happening.
I learn about all the tubes and machines.

It makes me feel a little less scared.

I hold Lucca's hand and we listen
to some of his favorite songs on my tablet.

He's awake some of the time, but he looks really tired. I brought his stuffed penguin from home and put it on his bed. Mom will spend the night at the hospital with him. Dad will come home with me.

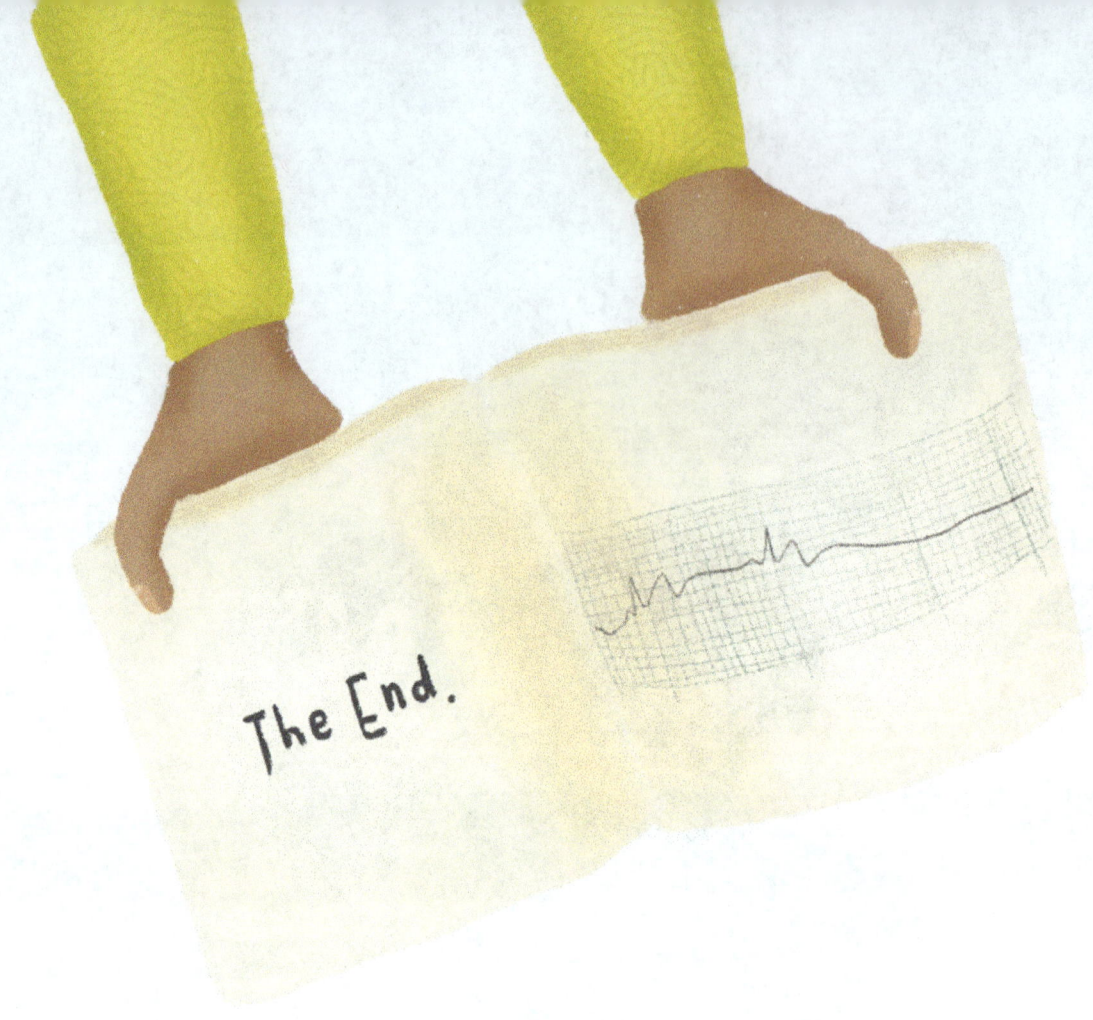

The next day my dad wakes me up.
He tells me my brother died.

I ask my mom how you know
if someone is really dead.

She says you know when their heart
stops beating, they stop breathing,
and you can't see
their chest going up and down.

They can no longer move, play, or talk.

*Parent Tip: Talk about concrete things such as skin color, lack of movement,
body temperature, etc.*

I feel terrible.

I cry and cry and cry.

Parent Tip: Sometimes kids cope well with distractions. It is common for young children to be sad one moment and ready to play or laugh the next. This is normal and appropriate though it can be unsettling for adults. Children may not spend the same amount of time thinking or processing events as grown-ups. Children being in and out of grief is normal and not disrespectful.

People start showing up at our house.
There are grandpas, grandmas, aunts, uncles, cousins,
and even some neighbors.
Some bring food. Some bring coffee.
Some just bring warm hugs.

Everyone looks sad.

My mom and dad
talk to me about the funeral.

A funeral is when family and friends
come together to remember the person
who has died.

Funerals often include music, speeches,
and prayers. This is also the last time
I will see my brother.

They ask if there is anything special
I would like to do or say to remember him.

Parent Tip: Here is a space to talk about your family's traditions and how you will remember/say goodbye to your loved one (i.e., a memorial, a viewing). Talking about where the body goes and stays (whether turned to ashes or buried), is important and will depend upon the child's age and questions. Talk about the remembrance spaces such as the cemetery, an urn, an altar and how these spaces can be decorated with flowers and mementos.

That's when I remember
what my math teacher, Mrs. Ortiz,
once told me.

Her mom loved collecting seashells
and treasures from the beach.

When her mom died,
Mrs. Ortiz looked through her mom's
beach collection and picked her favorites.

The rest she set in a basket
for everyone who came to the funeral.
She wanted everyone to take one
to remember her mom.

This gives me an idea.

My brother collected toy cars
and had a huge collection.
I want to share his collection
with people who loved him.

I can put them out
at the funeral so everyone
can have a small reminder
of him.

I'm keeping his favorite blue car
with the number 11.

My dad and grandpa
love this idea.

I have another idea.

I'll make a memory box.

I paint it green, then carefully add
other special things
that remind me of my brother . . .

. . . his lucky glow-in-the-dark marble,
his gray cozy beanie, a $2 bill,
a photo of us on the swings,
and a piece of his favorite grape bubble gum.

These things remind me of my brother.

What things remind you
of your brother or sister?

Maybe you can make a memory box too,
with his or her favorite things.

Parent Tip: Finding small jobs or ways to help kids remember their sibling is important. These can be artistic projects or a special ritual they create, like eating their favorite meal in their memory or going to their favorite place. It can be wearing a special color at the memorial or having a special photo, flower, or food displayed.

I will always miss my brother.

Parent Tip: Feel free to interchange words to make this narrative work with your family traditions, i.e., instead of visiting the cemetery you could suggest bringing out the urn or going to a place he loved.

Some days, I still feel upset.

Other days I feel happy,
and glad to play ball with my friends
at the park.

Some days, I feel extra sad.

When I feel like this, I talk with someone
I love, ask to visit my brother's grave,
listen to one of his favorite songs
or look at photos of him.

I will always be a big sister,
even if my little brother isn't here anymore.

I will always remember him
and I will always love him.

Parent Tip: Letting kids know it is okay to talk about their deceased loved ones is important and can help them throughout their grief journey, even if it is hard for the adults. If your family's belief tradition has an afterlife, this is the space to talk about it.

Acknowledgments

Five years ago this book was only a dream. It took my mom publishing three of her own books, and a lot of encouragement, to inspire me to write mine. Joy, this book would not exist without you. Your ability to turn words into art with attention to detail is unparalleled.

A very special thank you to the patients, families and staff members who live within these pages. You have given me lessons on grief and grace that I will carry with me always.

Thank you to all my editors and fellow Child Life Specialists who edited and encouraged me, especially, Eunice Kung, Cindy Schapiro, Samantha Johnson, Lynn Brock, Abbie Helman, Rachel Pedinoff, Keithra Ortiz, and Jane Reynolds. Thanks to Barbara Sourkes and Janae Dueck for their creativity and wisdom. Special thanks to Rita Avisa and Marta Montalvo-Kao for help with the translation of this book into Spanish.

Matias and Santino, los amo mucho, como un panucho. Santino, I hope you catch glimpses of your own childhood in these pages.

I'd like to extend a heartfelt thank you to Karen Mireau who took this book on as a special project, to ensure that grieving children would have the opportunity to read this story. I am forever grateful for your kindness.

Last, I would like to acknowledge the many people who asked about my book and cheered me on throughout my writing journey.

—Vanessa Ya Lopez
July 2024

About the Author

Vanessa Ya Lopez has been a Certified Child Life Specialist at Lucile Packard Children's Hospital, Stanford for 16 years. She also provides home visits through Coastal Kids Home Care, giving kids opportunities to play, explore and express themselves despite their illnesses.

Over the years, and after many experiences with pediatric deaths, she has gained skills to help children and teens confront death in an honest and compassionate way.

Vanessa received two bachelors degrees from the University of California, Irvine and a Masters in ECE from Mills College. She studied abroad in Costa Rica in 2003 and loves connecting and advocating for Spanish speaking families, especially new mothers.

Vanessa lives with her husband and son in the San Francisco Bay Area. She enjoys drinking Boba tea, reading, photography, beachcombing, hiking, finding hearts, waterfalls, tree swings, and banana slugs. This is her first book.

About the Illustrator

Joy Nicolas is a Certified Child Life Specialist who worked with the Hematology/Oncology population for four years. She recently started working per diem at Lucile Packard Children's Hospital, Stanford.

Most of Joy's illustrations are a reflection of the resilient and inspiring children she has supported with acute and chronic illnesses. It has been an honor for Joy to be present in the most vulnerable times of a child, especially at the end of life.

Joy holds a bachelor's degree from the University of California Irvine, a Masters in ECE from Mills College, and a certificate in children's book illustration from UCSD Extension.

Joy lives in the Bay Area, California, with her husband and son. Her favorite pastimes include floral arranging, reading, drawing, coffee dates, boxing, and hosting parties. This is Joy's first illustrated book.

To contact the Author
Vanessa Ya Lopez
please email:
yalopez@ymail.com

To order more copies of this book
please visit
Lulu.com
and Amazon.com

www.ingramcontent.com/pod-product-compliance
Lightning Source LLC
LaVergne TN
LVHW061344060426
835512LV00016B/2656